FLIGHT ATTENDANT

By William David Thomas

Reading Consultant: Susan Nations, M.Ed.,
author/literacy coach/consultant in literacy development

Gareth Stevens
Publishing

Please visit our web site at **www.garethstevens.com.**
For a free catalog describing Gareth Stevens Publishing's list of high-quality books, call 1-800-542-2595 (USA) or 1-800-387-3178 (Canada).
Gareth Stevens Publishing's fax: 1-877-542-2596

Library of Congress Cataloging-in-Publication Data
Thomas, William David
    Flight attendant / by William David Thomas.
      p. cm. — (Cool careers : on the go)
    Includes bibliographical references and index.
    ISBN-10: 1-4339-0003-3   ISBN-13: 978-1-4339-0003-7 (lib.bdg.)
    ISBN-10: 1-4339-0167-6   ISBN-13: 978-1-4339-0167-6 (softcover)
    1. Flight attendants—Vocational guidance—Juvenile literature. I. Title.
literature. I. Title.
    HD8039.A43.T56   2009
    387.7'42023—dc22   2008041639

This edition first published in 2009 by
Gareth Stevens Publishing
A Weekly Reader® Company
1 Reader's Digest Rd.
Pleasantville, NY 10570-7000 USA

Copyright © 2009 by Gareth Stevens, Inc.

Executive Managing Editor: Lisa M. Herrington
Creative Director: Lisa Donovan
Senior Editor: Barbara Bakowski
Editor: Joann Jovinelly
Designer: Paula Jo Smith
Photo Researcher: Kimberly Babbitt
Publisher: Keith Garton

Picture credits: Cover and title page: David Stluka/Getty Images; p. 5 David Lyons/Alamy; p. 6 AP Photo/Australia Transport Safety Bureau; p. 7 Jupiter Images; p. 8 Bettman/Corbis; p. 11 Scott Olson/Getty Images; p. 12 Digital Vision/Getty Images; p. 13 Richard Hutchings Photography; p. 15, 16 Benjamin Lowy/Corbis; p. 19 Raveendran/AFP/Getty Images; p. 20 Patrick Giardino/Corbis; p. 23 Najlah Feanny/Corbis; p. 24 A. Chederros/Getty Images; p. 26 Richard Hutchings Photography; p. 27 Courtesy of Amanda Kozlowski; p. 28 Anthony West/Corbis

Printed in the United States of America

1 2 3 4 5 6 7 8 9 10 09 08

CONTENTS

Words in the glossary appear in **bold** type the first time they are used in the text.

CHAPTER 1

FLIGHT PLAN

Most people only dream of traveling to distant cities like those they see on TV or in movies. Flight attendants get to see those places in person. They travel between cities, across countries, and around the world. Some joke about "living out of a suitcase," but most are excited about their jobs. After all, few careers offer as many travel options. If you want an on-the-go lifestyle that takes you to new heights, a career as a flight attendant might be right for you.

Jet-Setters!

For many flight attendants, the joy of their career is the chance to travel far from home. They can spend time in other countries, often for less money than a vacation would cost. Who wouldn't want a career with built-in vacations?

Flight attendants enjoy helping people. They help make travel comfortable and pleasant for passengers. Sometimes flight attendants have to cope with bumpy trips and last-minute schedule changes.

A flight attendant serves snacks and drinks to passengers.

Safe Travels

The most important part of the job is keeping people safe and informed. That was especially true on July 25, 2008. Passengers on a Qantas Airlines jumbo jet were heading to Australia. Suddenly, there was a loud bang.

The plane tipped to one side and started down. Bits of paper and plastic flew through the **cabin**. The air was being sucked out of the plane. An explosion had blown a hole in its side!

Within seconds, flight attendants responded to passengers' questions. They helped passengers put on **oxygen** masks. They kept people from panicking. "It was absolutely terrifying, but everyone was very calm," recalled passenger June Kane. Flight attendants explained that pilots needed to make an emergency landing to keep everyone safe.

After an explosion, this Qantas plane made an emergency landing. No one was hurt.

What Do Flight Attendants Do?

After safety, passenger comfort is the main focus of the job. Flight attendants help people who are elderly or who have disabilities to get on and off the plane. Flight attendants also serve drinks, snacks, and meals. They provide pillows, hand out magazines, and answer a lot of questions!

Flight attendants must stay calm during an emergency. Luckily, emergencies are rare. Flight attendants give instructions and help passengers with safety equipment. After an emergency landing, they get everyone out of the aircraft. They may need to give first aid to injured people.

A flight attendant shows passengers how to put on an oxygen mask.

The First Flight Attendants

Passengers began flying on airplanes in the 1920s. On some flights, men called stewards helped passengers with their luggage. In 1930, a nurse named Ellen Church (left) contacted Boeing Air Transport. She said more passengers would fly if they felt safer. Church suggested that Boeing place nurses on board airplanes. Church's idea was successful. Soon, other airlines began hiring "flying nurses," called stewardesses.

What You'll Need

To work as a flight attendant in the United States, you must be an American citizen. You must be at least 18 years old (some airlines require you to be 21). Flight attendants need to have a high school diploma. Some larger airlines prefer applicants who have taken college classes, too. Airlines also have specific rules about height and eyesight. Flight attendants must be able to see the entire cabin and reach overhead storage bins.

How to Become a Flight Attendant

When seeking a job as a flight attendant, you must fill out an **application**. You may be called for an **interview**. If you are selected, the airline will look at your records. They will check to see if you were born in the United States. They will also check your work history. After a successful background check, you will begin training. The training program usually lasts several weeks. It includes both classroom and hands-on safety training.

Could You Be a Flight Attendant?

If you think you'd like to be a flight attendant, ask yourself these questions:

- Do you love to travel?
- Do you like to fly?
- Do you mind being away from home?
- Can you keep calm in an emergency?
- Can you be friendly and polite to people who are not?
- Are you organized and good at keeping records?
- Do you respect rules?

If so, you might soar as a flight attendant!

CHAPTER 2

BOARDING PASS

Most people would love a job that often lets them fly for free. A career as a flight attendant has other perks, too, such as low-cost air travel for family members.

Being a flight attendant is rewarding. But the job can also be tiring. The hours are long. Schedules may change with little notice. When flights are delayed, flight attendants sometimes must stay overnight far from home. Flights may be canceled because of poor weather conditions or problems with aircraft.

Standing Out

Each year, thousands of men and women seek jobs as flight attendants. Competition for those jobs is tough. All people who have a high school diploma can apply. Most large airlines prefer two or four years of college. Experience dealing with the public in a setting such as a restaurant or a hotel is helpful.

Two flight attendants head for work at O'Hare Airport, in Chicago, Illinois.

What's Your Code?

Every airport has a three-letter code name used by airlines. Some, such as DAL (for Dallas, Texas), are easy to remember. The code for Pittsburgh, Pennsylvania, is PIT. Other codes are harder. O'Hare Airport in Chicago, Illinois, is known as ORD. Spokane, Washington, has the code name GEG. Flight attendants in the United States must learn nearly 300 codes!

Speaking a foreign language is also a bonus. Airlines fly around the world. They have passengers who speak many languages. They need flight attendants who can communicate quickly and easily. Some airlines hire only people who speak two or more languages.

A few flight attendant positions are also available on private or corporate planes. Those jobs sometimes offer the ability to meet celebrities, politicians, or famous athletes. Since gourmet meals are prepared aboard private flights, previous work experience in fine restaurants is a plus.

Passengers come from many different countries. Flight attendants who speak more than one language are in demand.

Babies in the Air

BABY ON BOARD

British Airways reports that at least one baby is born on their flights nearly every year. In 2007, a Delta passenger flying from Germany to the United States went into labor. Flight attendants asked for help. Two doctors were on board. They helped the woman deliver a baby boy. Flight attendants are trained for medical emergencies, and airplanes carry medical kits. Still, they are happy to have professional help.

Training for Takeoff

Flight attendant training lasts from four to six weeks. There is a lot to learn, so the hours are long. Instruction is usually given ten hours a day, six days a week. Trainees study the airline's history. They learn the rules flight attendants must follow. They also find out how flight attendants are chosen for different trips.

During in-flight training, new flight attendants learn how to safely open and close airplane doors. They

Flight attendants must know how to open and close aircraft doors.

SALIDA
EXIT

PELIGRO
NO ABRA LA PUERTA
SI LA LUZ ROJA DE ADVERTENCIA
ENSENDIDA INTERMITENTE
(CABINA PRESURIZADA)

DANGER
DO NOT OPEN DOOR
IF RED WARNING LIGHT IS FLASHING
(CABIN PRESSURIZED)

practice getting ready for takeoff and landing. They serve drinks, snacks, and meals. Experienced flight attendants show trainees the best ways to work with passengers. Older adults, small children, and grumpy passengers may need more attention.

Flight attendants must also keep accurate records. Daily logs are kept for items sold on board. Special forms are also filled out when flights go to or return from other countries.

Saving Lives

The most important part of training is learning how to practice safety in any situation. "Passengers think we're here to serve them drinks," said one flight attendant. "But we're really here to save their lives."

The FAA and the FAR

The Federal Aviation Administration (FAA) is part of the U.S. government. The FAA writes the Federal Airline Regulations (FAR). Those rules must be followed by airlines, pilots, and flight attendants. The FAR tell how many flight attendants must be on each type of airplane. They require each flight attendant to have a flashlight at all times. Crews must be able to **evacuate** a fully loaded airplane in 90 seconds or less, using only half of the exits.

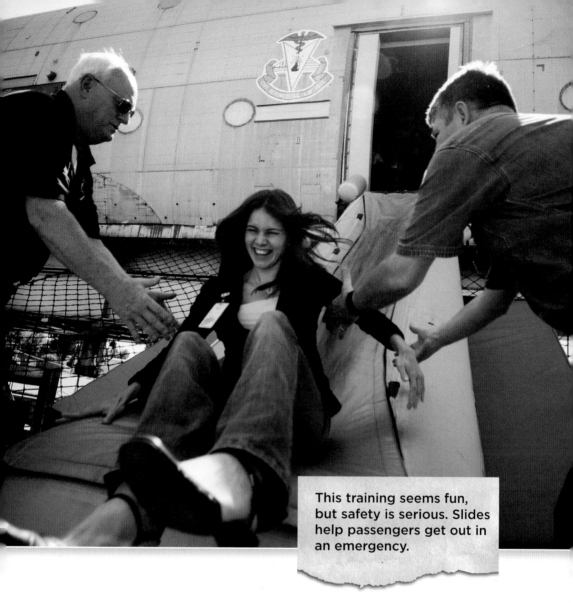

This training seems fun, but safety is serious. Slides help passengers get out in an emergency.

Make an Escape!

Emergency training takes place on full-sized models of real aircraft. Flight attendants practice using fire extinguishers. They learn how to get injured passengers out of a plane. They also practice using the escape slides that are inside airplane doors.

These flight attendants train for an emergency landing in water.

Lights Out

All flight attendants must learn first aid and **CPR**. Different kinds of airplanes have different firefighting and emergency medical equipment on board. Flight attendants are tested on the location of each item on each kind of airplane. They must be able to find that equipment quickly and use it correctly, even in the dark.

Splash Down!

Training always includes instructions for water landings. Those skills are taught in a large swimming pool. Flight

attendants learn how to jump into the water, inflate a life raft, and rescue passengers. They are also taught how to use signaling equipment to call rescue boats and other aircraft.

Getting Wings

At the end of training, flight attendants are fitted for a uniform. They pay for the clothes, but the cost can be taken out of future paychecks a little bit at a time. Once they have their uniforms and airline ID badges, they're ready to take off!

Paying Dues

Nearly all flight attendants are members of an organization called a **union**. Members pay dues, and union officials represent them within the airline. The union wants its members to have good pay, health care, and safe working conditions. The Air Line Stewardesses Association was the first union for flight attendants. It was started in 1945 by United Airlines flight attendant Ada Brown. Today, there are seven flight attendant unions in North America. The largest, the Association of Professional Flight Attendants, had about 19,000 members in 2008.

CHAPTER 3
TAKEOFF

At first, a new flight attendant is closely supervised. An experienced flight attendant stays with him or her. Official regulations require at least five hours of supervised flight time.

Ready to Go!

New flight attendants are nearly always placed on reserve. That means they fill in for people who are sick or have emergencies. Reserve flight attendants must be ready to go at a moment's notice. Often, they must go to the airport in uniform and wait to be called if they are needed.

Bidding

Each month, every airline posts a **bid package**. This is a list of all flights scheduled for the coming month. Flight attendants must bid, or sign up, for the flights they want. If several people want the same flight, it goes to the person with the most **seniority**. Seniority is based on the length of time a person has worked for the airline. "Seniority dictates which trips you fly [and] what position you work in the aircraft," explained one former flight attendant.

An in-flight supervisor
(left) coaches a new
flight attendant.

Crew Briefing

Flight attendants must be at the airport at least one
hour before a flight leaves. They must check in at the
airline office, in uniform, with their suitcases packed.
Before each flight, there is a crew **briefing**. The crew

Home Base

Airlines are located in **hub cities**, such as New
York and Chicago. Many flight attendants share
living spaces near hub city airports. Several flight
attendants may share the cost for one apartment or
house. They save money and have a place to stay
during short **layovers**, or rest periods.

members review assignments for the flight. They get a list of passengers with disabilities or special needs.

Flight attendants board the plane about 45 minutes before takeoff. They store their suitcases in a special area. Next, they check all safety equipment to make sure it is ready for use. As passengers arrive, flight attendants help them find their seats and store bags.

Ready for Takeoff

When everyone is on board, flight attendants must close, lock, and check all doors. They show passengers safety gear. That includes seat belts, emergency exits,

A flight attendant shows passengers how to work the safety belts.

After 9/11

After the terrorist attacks of September 11, 2001, flight attendant training and practices changed. Flight attendants now get self-defense training. They are also taught to guard their uniforms and airline ID badges carefully. They must protect official clothing and IDs from being stolen. Flight attendants are also taught not to allow passengers to stand near the bathrooms, kitchen, or **cockpit**. The cockpit door is locked and barred. Flight attendants must use special codes to enter that area.

oxygen masks, and life vests. Flight attendants use hand signals to point out emergency equipment and exits. On some planes, this information is presented in a video.

The plane starts to **taxi**, or move slowly down the runway. Flight attendants walk up and down the aisles. They make sure all passengers have fastened their seat belts. They check that all storage bins are closed. They also remind passengers to turn off cell phones and other electronic devices. Those items can sometimes disrupt the plane's communication system.

Just before takeoff, flight attendants sit in special fold-down seats. Those seats spring out of the way when they are not in use. Like passengers, flight attendants must stay seated and belted until the plane stops climbing. When the plane levels off, they get back to work.

CHAPTER 4

IN FLIGHT

The crew's first in-flight job is usually setting up the beverage cart. Flight attendants move through the plane to serve passengers their choice of drinks. Coffee, soft drinks, and other beverages are available on most flights. Some drinks must be purchased. Flight attendants keep track of the drinks sold and the money collected.

Meals on Wheels

If the flight is a long one, passengers are sometimes served a meal. Some flight attendants are assigned to the **galley**, or kitchen. While passengers are boarding, the galley workers make sure there are enough meals on board. The galley crew heats the meals in a special oven. Other flight attendants push carts down the aisles to deliver meals to passengers. On shorter flights, or when full meals are not offered, flight attendants serve pre-made items. Those are sealed containers of prepared food such as salads, sandwiches, and snacks that can be given out quickly and easily.

Once all refreshments and meals have been served, flight attendants start down the aisles

What's for breakfast? Passengers on this morning flight enjoy a meal.

again. They carry plastic trash bags to collect napkins, plates, cans, and empty cups. Everything must be put away before the plane lands.

Ready for Landing

Before the plane lands, flight attendants make announcements. They tell passengers about the weather and **connecting flights**. As the plane

starts down, flight attendants check seat belts and storage bins. Then they buckle themselves into seats for landing.

When the plane reaches the gate, flight attendants open the doors. They help passengers exit. Then they check the cabin for items that were left behind. The **ground crew** may deliver more drinks, meals, and other supplies. Flight attendants record and store those items. Then it's time to for them greet new passengers for the next flight.

Layover

There are limits to the number of hours air crews can work without stopping. Longer flights often have a layover. It may be several hours, overnight, or a full day. Flight attendants gather their suitcases and head for a place to rest. They eat, sleep, shower, and change clothes. Soon they must head back to the airport. They are on the go again!

Speaking of Airplanes

New flight attendants have to learn the language of airplanes.

aft: toward the back of a plane

bulkhead: a wall that divides sections of an airplane

coach: the section of seats at the rear of an airplane

first class: larger, more costly section of seats at the front of an airplane

forward: toward the front of a plane

fuselage: the body of an airplane (without the wings or tail)

gate: an area where passengers get on or off a plane at an airport

CHAPTER 5

A SMOOTH LANDING

Men and women of all ages and backgrounds now work as flight attendants. In fact, most airlines search for people from a variety of cultures to fill those jobs. That is because people from different cultures often speak more than one language.

Another bonus of working as a flight attendant is a flexible schedule. Today's flight attendants may work full time or part time. If they wish, they can work fewer flights and spend more time with their families.

This flight attendant heads for a hotel and some well-deserved rest.

On the Job: Flight Attendant Amanda Kozlowski

Amanda Kozlowski has been a flight attendant for Southwest Airlines for four years.

Q: Why did you become a flight attendant?

Kozlowski: A friend of my mom had been a flight attendant. She was always saying how cool it was, so I thought I'd try it.

Q: What was your training like?

Kozlowski: I had to go to Dallas, Texas. We worked twelve hours a day, six days a week, for four and a half weeks.

Q: Where have you flown?

Kozlowski: I've flown all over the United States. Southwest serves about seventy cities, and I've been to all but two of them.

Q: What's the best thing about being a flight attendant?

Kozlowski: The best thing about my job is being able to visit so many different places.

Q: What's the hardest part of the job?

Kozlowski: Traveling is tiring. I'm away from home a lot.

Q: What experience stands out to you most as a flight attendant?

Kozlowski: During my first year, we flew into O'Hare [Chicago] in a terrible snowstorm. The plane landing right behind us slid off the runway, passed through a fence, and hit a car. The whole airport shut down for a while.

Q: What would you tell young people who are thinking about becoming flight attendants?

Kozlowski: It takes a lot of dedication, but it's a great experience.

Making a Difference

Antonio D'Auria is a flight attendant for Delta Airlines. He has no children, but 150 kids call him "Father." They live in an orphanage in Ghana, West Africa. Antonio visited it once during a flight layover. "I took a small bag of goodies with me," he said. "That became a suitcase, and then more and more." Now other flight attendants give him clothes, books, and food to take to the children. Antonio says, "I get paid to fly. Why not make a difference in the lives of some children who are not so fortunate?"

The Sky's the Limit

Flight attendants are always in motion, flying across the country or around the world. Some flight attendants move into other jobs, too. They may train new flight attendants. A few become in-flight supervisors. Former flight attendants may do bidding and work scheduling, too.

No matter where they are heading, flight attendants must keep people informed and safe. Most of all, they do their best to make a passenger's flight a happy one. If you like being on the go, consider testing your wings as a flight attendant.

Flight attendants make sure passengers have a smooth, safe ride.

Career Fact File

FLIGHT ATTENDANT

OUTLOOK

- About 97,000 flight attendants currently work for commercial and private companies in the United States. By 2016, about 107,000 jobs will be available.

WHAT YOU'LL DO

- The first duty of all flight attendants is passenger safety. They help passengers who are sick or who have disabilities. Flight attendants guide everyone out of the aircraft in an emergency.

- Flight attendants provide passengers with pillows, blankets, and information about their flight and connecting flights.

- On flights outside the United States, they provide more detailed information or translate foreign languages.

- Flight attendants serve drinks and snacks to passengers. On long flights, they may serve meals. Flight attendants also collect money, make change, and keep records of all sales.

WHAT YOU'LL NEED

- Flight attendants working for U.S. airlines must be citizens of the United States.

- Flight attendants are required to have a high school diploma. Most airlines prefer to hire people with at least some college education.

- Flight attendants must pass a background check. Their records and work history will be investigated.

- Airlines have height and weight guidelines and rules about dress and personal appearance.

WHAT YOU'LL EARN

- New flight attendants earn about $30,000. The most experienced flight attendants earn as much as $102,000.

Source: U.S. Department of Labor, Bureau of Labor Statistics

x

GLOSSARY

application — papers that must be filled out when seeking a job

bid package — a list of all flights scheduled for the coming month; flight attendants must bid for, or request, the flights they want

briefing — a meeting where information is given out

cabin — the part of an airplane where passengers sit

cockpit — the front of the airplane where the pilot and copilot control the aircraft

connecting flights — flights that take you from one city to the city you want to reach

CPR — cardiopulmonary resuscitation; a way to restart a person's heartbeat and breathing if they have stopped

evacuate — to quickly leave a place because of an emergency

galley — the kitchen area on an airplane

ground crew — airport workers who move baggage and bring fuel and supplies to airplanes

hub cities — cities where most airline flights begin and end

interview — a meeting in which a person is questioned, often to see if he or she should be given a job

layovers — rest periods between flights for flight attendants, pilots, and crew

oxygen — a gas that is part of the air we breathe; humans need oxygen to stay alive

seniority — length of time with a company

taxi — to move slowly along the ground

union — an organization that helps workers get better benefits, wages, and working conditions; members pay dues to belong to a union

TO FIND OUT MORE

Books

Cool Careers Without College for People Who Love to Travel.
Cool Careers Without College (series). Simone Payment
(Rosen Publishing, 2003)

Flight. Secret Worlds (series). Reg G. Grant and Michael Allaby
(DK Publishing, 2003)

Into the Air: An Illustrated Timeline of Flight. Ryan Ann Hunter
(National Geographic Children's Books, 2003)

Web Sites

Airport Codes
www.airportcitycodes.com
Find the three-letter code for the airport nearest you!

Federal Aviation Administration (FAA)
www.faa.gov/jobs
Search the jobs page of the FAA.

Flight Attendant Facts
*www.flightattendantfacts.com/flight_attendant/
flight_attendant_life.html*
Check out a day in the life of a U.S. flight attendant!

How Stuff Works
www.science.howstuffworks.com/airline-crew.htm
Find out how pilots and flight attendants work.

Publisher's note to educators and parents: Our editors have carefully reviewed these web sites to ensure that they are suitable for children. Many web sites change frequently, however, and we cannot guarantee that a site's future contents will continue to meet our high standards of quality and educational value. Be advised that children should be closely supervised whenever they access the Internet.

INDEX

About the Author

William David Thomas lives in Rochester, New York. In his career, Bill has written software documentation, magazine articles, training programs, annual reports, books for children, a few poems, and lots of letters. Bill claims he was once the king of Fiji but gave up the throne to pursue a career as a relief pitcher. It's not true.